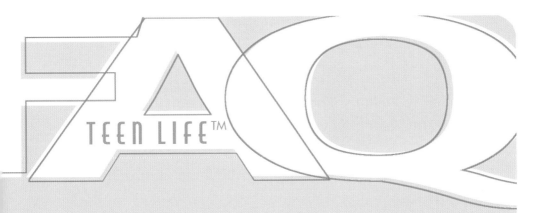

TEEN LIFE™

FREQUENTLY ASKED QUESTIONS ABOUT

When a Friend Dies

Corona
Brezina

ROSEN
PUBLISHING®

New York

Published in 2008 by The Rosen Publishing Group, Inc.
29 East 21st Street, New York, NY 10010

Library of Congress Cataloging-in-Publication Data

Brezina, Corona.
Frequently asked questions about when a friend dies / Corona Brezina—1st ed.
   p. cm.—(FAQ: teen life)
Includes bibliographical references and index.
ISBN-13: 978-1-4042-1935-9
ISBN-10: 1-4042-1935-8
1. Grief in adolescence. 2. Bereavement in adolescence. 3. Teenagers and death. I. Title.
BF724.3.G73B74 2007
155.9'37—dc22

2006101198

Manufactured in the United States of America

Contents

Introduction 4

1
What Happens
When a
Friend Dies? 7

2
What Is Grief? 16

3
How Can I
Cope with Grief? 25

4
What Can
People Do to
Reconnect? 38

5
When Will
I Recover? 46

Glossary 56
For More Information 58
For Further Reading 60
Bibliography 61
Index 62

Introduction

The death of a child or teenager is always a tragedy. A part of us feels that such a death goes against the natural cycles of life. The death of an elderly relative or acquaintance evokes grief and loss, but the bereaved can usually take comfort in memories of a long and happy life. When a young person dies, there is a sense that a life has been cut short.

The death of a friend is a particularly wrenching experience. Feelings of grief and loss may be heightened if the circumstances of death were traumatic, as when the death was the result of suicide, a car accident, a medical condition, or violence. Young people often have a special blind spot when it comes to understanding death. As a teenager, it is easy to feel as if you are going to live forever. You may feel as if you are invincible, and it is hard to imagine that death can intrude on your life.

Adolescence is a time of growth and transition, a period when relationships, bodies, and attitudes are in a state of change. It is shocking to bear the loss of a friend in the midst of maturing and looking toward the future. You may find it agonizing to think that your friend will no longer be with you to share the experiences of growing up. It is even harder because adults do not always know how to treat a grieving teen. Teenagers cannot be comforted in the same way as younger children; neither can they be expected to cope with

Dealing with the death of a friend is always hard. It is especially difficult when you are young and unfamiliar with the strong emotions that accompany loss.

death in the same way as adults. Have you ever noticed that conversations about death and dying frequently stop when a young person enters the room? Adults may prevent young people from going to funerals and cemeteries, or from viewing the body of a deceased friend. Parents have the best intentions and take these steps to protect their children's feelings, but such precautions can sometimes lead to teens feeling isolated in their grief.

Studies show that young people need to know the facts about death, and they need to say good-bye to the person who has died. Talking about death and attending ceremonies for the dead are not harmful to young people. Although these rituals can be upsetting, they teach you a difficult truth about life and how to cope with the grief that comes with losing a loved one.

You might feel a different kind of grief depending on your relationship with your friend. If you knew your friend since grade school, you may feel that you've lost a link to your own past. If the person was your boyfriend or girlfriend, you may feel that you've lost your hopes and dreams for the future. When a loved one dies, people often say, "I feel like a part of me has died, too." Even if the deceased was not a close friend, it's normal to grieve. It's traumatizing to realize that someone who was part of your life—maybe someone you admired from afar—is gone forever.

This may be your first experience with personal loss and grief. If so, you probably gave little thought to the phenomenon of grief before the death of your friend. The depth and intensity of your grief will come as a shock to you, as it is a painful and draining experience. When you are grieving, you find it hard to believe that you will ever feel happy again. Don't forget, though, that there are resources available to help teens and young people cope with grief. It will take time, but you will eventually attain healing and acceptance of your loss, and you'll find the strength to look toward the future.

one

WHAT HAPPENS WHEN A FRIEND DIES?

There is no "right" reaction to the loss of a friend. Some people dissolve into tears, while others wonder if there is something wrong with them because they cannot cry at all. You may channel your sense of loss by keeping yourself constantly occupied. On the other hand, you might find yourself unable to concentrate or get anything done. People often feel a sense of numbness and disbelief in the hours and days after experiencing a loss. All of these emotions are normal. It is always a shock when a friend dies.

Different Deaths, Different Emotions

Whether it happens unexpectedly or as the result of a long illness, there is no way you can truly prepare yourself for

Shock, disbelief, intense anger, fear, and frustration—these are all possible emotional reactions to the news that a friend has died.

the flood of emotions you experience when you hear the news. In one moment, your world is changed.

Death from a Sudden Illness

When a friend dies from a sudden illness, it can be more of a shock than an illness that progresses slowly. The emotions that accompany the ordeal come quickly and intensely.

On the other hand, death from an illness that is unexpected and brief can be a blessing, especially if the ailment is painful to the sufferer. The suddenness shortens the time that the sick person has to suffer, as well as the time you witness the suffering.

Death from a Gradual Illness

You may react differently to an illness that does not occur suddenly. You may know someone who has an illness that is slowly getting worse. If you are in this kind of situation, you may experience an even more confusing variety of emotions. Some days may bring hope that is dashed by a sudden downturn in your friend's health. Depending on the length of the dying process, these emotions may last for a longer period of time, potentially making the loss even more painful.

Terminal Illness

Cancer and some other diseases can be terminal. When people have an illness that can't be cured, they may stay in the hospital, go home, or go to live their last days in a hospice (a place for people with terminal illnesses). If your sick friend needs medical attention, he or she must stay in the hospital.

A terminally ill person may be able to go home to stay with family. Even though he or she is dying, being at home can make him or her feel better. Being in familiar surroundings, close to the people he or she loves, is comforting. When a dying person has accepted the possibility of his or her own death, however, he or she might wish to see fewer people for a while, or even be alone. You should understand that this is a natural reaction to the situation. It does not mean that your dying friend doesn't care about you or has rejected you.

If your friend is in a hospice, you will be allowed to visit. Doctors, nurses, and counselors at a hospice are trained to work with patients who are dying. They try to make the dying person as comfortable as possible. They also work with the patient's friends and families. They are trained to help people deal with their feelings of sadness.

No one, including the doctors, knows when a patient is going to die. Not knowing this can be painful and confusing. There will be good days, when your sick friend seems to be recovering. In terminal cases, the good days will not last. But your company can make the good days even better.

Spending time with a terminally ill friend can be difficult and scary. But when you look back on that time, you will be glad you were there for your friend.

Death from Violence

Violent death provokes extremely powerful feelings because it is usually unexpected and seems so senseless. When a friend dies a violent death, you are reminded about your own mortality. The world does not seem as secure or as safe as it once did. You may be sad about the death but worried about yourself at the same time. No one is immune to violence and tragedy. It can affect anyone at any time. Violent death is frightening because it reminds everyone that life can be over in an instant.

You'll feel many different emotions when someone you know dies by violence. You may feel guilty that you are still alive, grateful that you weren't the victim, stunned and saddened by the loss of someone you loved, angry about how he or she died, and/or afraid of the dangers that you now see lurking around you.

Death by Suicide

Perhaps the most difficult kind of death to deal with is death by suicide. When a young person takes his or her own life, there are so many questions left unanswered. Friends are left to think about the awful pain the person must have been experiencing, and sometimes they wonder whether their own actions or words had anything to do with the suicide. If you are lucky, you'll never be affected by this type of tragedy, but suicide among young people is a serious concern.

Relying on Others

It is important for you to remember that you are not alone in your grieving. In the days following the death of your friend, there will be occasions when friends, family, and community come together for mourning and remembrance. These rituals and gatherings are a chance to say good-bye to loved ones and offer support for each other.

Many schools immediately offer grief counseling after the death of a student. This is usually directed by professionals who have experience in helping young people deal with tragedy. They may be able to help you cope with your initial reaction to the loss of your friend. If not, you can also meet with a private psychologist or psychotherapist to talk about your concerns.

Funerals and Other Rituals

In the days following the death, you will probably attend one or more rituals, formal or informal, to remember your friend. Rituals are a way to lay the dead to rest and begin the healing process for the living. At the same time, they give us a chance to reaffirm our ties to family and community.

Different cultures and religious faiths have their own traditions for honoring the dead, many of them with ancient roots. If your friend is Christian, his or her family may organize a wake. A Jewish family will sit shiva following a death: they will remain at home for a period of three to seven days and receive callers offering condolences. Humanistic services, which avoid religious references, are sometimes less formal and more personal than conventional ceremonies. There may also be a burial service in the cemetery.

The most common ritual of passage is the funeral. It is the time when family, friends, and community gather to say good-bye.

A funeral marks the end of a life. It also gives the living an opportunity to fully grieve for the person they have lost.

This is a chance for you to pay respects to the friend who was so important to you in life. Most people find comfort in coming together to recognize a very special person who touched the lives of everyone present. At funerals, people can openly express their grief. Everybody cries, hugs each other, and shares memories of the deceased. You might be surprised to find yourself smiling and laughing at some of the stories about your friend.

Entering Grief

The funeral is an important part of the grieving process. It is sometimes pointed out that funerals are really for the living. The deceased is laid to rest, and the living must begin to work through their grief. Even the custom of viewing the body is believed to help the healing process. Mourners are forced to face the reality of death. You might have said, "I can't believe he's really gone!" after the death of your friend. Funerals help people to accept that the person is truly gone and to move on to the next stage of healing.

As a teenager, this may be your first experience with death and its aftermath. You may feel stunned by the intensity of your grief. There is no way you can banish your pain, but for some people, it helps to take part in the funeral and assist with preparations. If you don't know much about the usual customs of funerals, talk with your parents and ask for advice on how you could participate. It is traditional to send flowers for a funeral. You may have a chance during the ceremony to share a memory or read a selection that you think your friend would appreciate. Family and friends often bring food to share on the day of the funeral.

Death rites vary around the world. In Hindu culture, a wooden funeral pyre is set alight to cremate the body of the deceased.

Don't isolate yourself from family and friends after the death of a friend. It is normal for people to need solitude in their grief, but reaching out to others—to offer and to receive comfort—is also important. You might feel that nobody else could be hurting as much as you are. Funerals and other rituals give you a chance to share your grief with others. Your pain won't stop, but these gatherings will give you strength and reassurance as you begin to move through the stages of grief and recovery.

two

WHAT IS GRIEF?

When we suffer a loss, we grieve. Grief is not a choice. It is the normal emotional response to a loss. Everybody experiences grief differently. It is akin to pain, suffering, or anguish. We feel twinges of grief if a friend moves away, when a relationship breaks apart, and at high school graduation. Grief is most intense after a major loss, such as the death of a friend. You should accept that it is a natural process and that it will take some time for you to work through your grief. It is not healthy for you to try to bottle up grief. Sooner or later, it will bubble out, with physical and psychological consequences.

The Five Stages of Grief

Grief brings an initial torrent of strong feelings, and different emotions arise as time passes. In her book *On Grief and*

Typically, the first stage of grief begins with shock and disbelief. During this time, it is very difficult to accept the reality of your friend's death.

Grieving, psychiatrist Elisabeth Kübler-Ross identifies five stages of grief: denial, anger, bargaining, depression/despair, and acceptance. As you read these, remember that there is no formula for grief—other psychiatrists have advanced different theories on grief recovery. These are merely stages that many people experience after a loss. You may not experience them in sequence or go through all of these stages.

Denial. When you first hear of your friend's death, the thought might go through your mind that it must be a mistake. Even when you have accepted the fact, you may feel numb. You might find yourself absently picking up the phone to call your friend or talking about him or her in the present tense. It takes time for you to register the reality of your loss.

Anger. People often work out some of their pain through anger. You might feel angry at your friend for leaving you alone or for not being more careful. You might blame doctors, friends, family, and even yourself for not preventing your friend's death. You may feel angry at God for allowing it to happen. Try to find an outlet for your anger without hurting the people close to you. Talk through your anger (or ventilate it appropriately by punching a pillow or writing a letter that you won't send). Don't take it out on others.

Bargaining. Kübler-Ross describes bargaining as a stage that begins before someone dies. It is an attempt to negotiate your way out of loss and to avoid acknowledging the reality of loss. Bargaining is closely linked with guilt and regret, which are both tendencies to dwell on "What if . . .?" and "If only . . ." instead of accepting loss and moving on. Teens, especially, tend to be overly self-critical. As much as possible, you must come to terms with your feelings of guilt and regret. Recognize that there is no benefit in revisiting every past choice, and try to forgive yourself for any hurtful behavior left unresolved.

Depression/Despair. After the reality of your friend's death has sunk in completely, you may feel overwhelmed with lethargy and hopelessness. Although it is painful to endure,

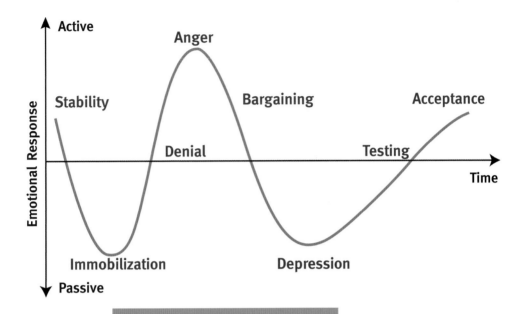

As this chart shows, the stages of grief are like an emotional roller coaster. According to most experts, it is important to pass through each stage on the way to acceptance.

this bereavement depression is a normal part of the grieving process. This is the point where it might feel like you can't imagine going on without your friend. Remember that this is an emotion that will pass. Try to take things one day at a time. Talk to friends and family about what you are feeling.

Acceptance. In time, you will readjust to life without your friend. This does not mean that you no longer feel a sense of loss. You will still have days when your sadness returns. The death of your friend has changed your world. In this

The stages of grief do not always adhere to a strict formula. Some people may remain depressed longer than others.

final stage of healing, though, you will come to terms with your loss and begin to look to the future once again.

Grieving Is Personal

Don't worry if your emotions following the loss of a friend do not fit neatly into one of these five categories. The four stages leading to acceptance are common responses to loss, but people generally feel a widely varying range of emotions after a friend or loved one has died. It's normal to experience a flood of emotions, some of them conflicting or unexpected. You might feel relief if the death followed an illness, and then feel guilty for being relieved. You may feel nervous or fearful. You might feel jealous of people who have not had their lives disrupted by a loss or who seem to be handling their grief much more easily. You may feel panic at the prospect of handling all of the changes in your life. Guilt is another common reaction to death. Survivors often question themselves about how they might have prevented the death. There is no single "right" way to feel after the death of a friend.

There is also no fixed timetable for grieving. Your friends and family might say to you, "Isn't it time for you to move on?" You may ask yourself the same question and worry that your grief isn't normal. It could take a few months for you to reach acceptance of your loss. It could even take a few years.

You might wonder during the grieving process if you will ever feel "normal" again. Maybe you can't imagine life returning to what it had been before the death of your friend. Remember, though, that what is "normal" in your life naturally shifts as you

Myths and Facts
About Grief

 There's no way my family and friends could ever understand how I'm feeling. Fact ➡ Your friends and family understand that you're grieving, and grief is different for everybody. Still, they probably have some understanding of your thoughts and emotions. Share your feelings with a friend or family member—it might help the both of you.

 You should get over it. Fact ➡ You can't choose to "get over" the death of a friend. In time, you will work through your grief and return to your everyday activities. You may sometimes feel pangs of loss, even after you have come to terms with the death of your friend.

 It isn't as bad for you since you aren't part of the family. Fact ➡ Coping with loss is a wrenching and painful experience, regardless of blood ties. Friendship and family ties are extremely close bonds. It's natural to feel intense grief for a friend.

Family members and others who have experienced loss can provide comfort when a friend has died.

You really shouldn't feel that way. Fact ➡ There's no "right" way to grieve. Everybody experiences the grieving process differently. You will probably feel a wide range of emotions as you work through your grief.

 It should have been you, instead of the person who died. Fact ➡ It is common to feel guilty about being alive when someone close to you has died. Death brings a lot of confusing feelings that need to be worked through, then let go.

mature and the world around you changes. The death of your friend was a sudden, traumatic occurrence in your life. You will return to "normal," but it may feel like a different sense of "normal" than before your loss.

three

HOW CAN I COPE WITH GRIEF?

Even during the process of grieving, life goes on. You might not feel ready to return to school, but you cannot put off your responsibilities for too long. At first, it might be hard to face your friends and teachers. You might have trouble concentrating and juggling school, family life, and extracurricular activities. It might seem that you've changed and that everything is different now that your friend is gone.

As you get back to your daily routine, pay attention to your physical and emotional well-being. Don't allow yourself to become so consumed with grief that it damages your health.

Grief can be draining. Some people find themselves sleeping far more than is usual. On the other hand, you may find that you have trouble getting to sleep. Make an effort to address your problem. Try drinking herbal tea or taking a bath before bedtime. Find

Grief can make it impossible to return to your regular schedule. Classes and other everyday activities might not seem important to you anymore.

a solution that works for you—exercise, music, light reading, or television before going to sleep might help.

Keep up your energy by eating a healthy diet. People often find that grief takes away their interest in food. If you cannot manage to sit down to an entire meal, try eating smaller amounts more often. Keep healthy snacks handy to grab throughout the day.

If you do not find a way to deal with your grief, it can take a heavy emotional toll on you. Teens tend to internalize their grief, or keep it inside. Sometimes this leads friends and family to believe that the teen isn't having any problems handling grief. Other times, though, they recognize that the teen has put up an emotional barricade. Even if it hurts, try to share your thoughts and feelings with someone. If you cannot talk with those who are close to you, seek out someone else you trust, such as a counselor, teacher, or church leader.

What NOT to Do

Instead of concealing their sense of loss, people sometimes demonstrate their grief with reckless or self-destructive behavior. This is especially true of teenagers, who may be stunned by their first close experience with death. The temptation is to live dangerously in order to defy death and act out emotions. Risky behavior, like driving recklessly or getting into fights, won't resolve your grief.

Also, in the days following your friend's death, you might be tempted to turn to alcohol or drugs to forget your problems, feel happy, or stop feeling altogether. But drinking alcohol or taking drugs to numb yourself actually intensifies your bad feelings. Avoid the temptation to take stimulants, or "uppers"—such as cocaine or speed—to battle the low energy that people often feel when grieving. You will only feel worse after you come down, or "crash," from a high. Taking drugs creates more problems by suppressing the feelings that come back even stronger when the drug wears off.

Don't try to use sex to end your loneliness. Having sex for the wrong reasons will only lead to more hurt.

Among Friends

In addition to looking after your own well-being, you will have to reestablish connections with friends on your path to healing. It might seem like your relationships with friends have changed since the death of your friend. You may feel like you're not exactly the same person you were before your loss. This is somewhat true, as we grow and change with each life experience. Sometimes people who have experienced a loss are afraid to let a friend get too close because they're afraid that they might lose that friend, too. As time passes, it should become easier to reach out to others.

Conversations may seem awkward when you first return to school. It's hard to know what to say to someone who is grieving. If your friend was a member of your close circle of friends, all of you will feel his or her absence in class and at social gatherings. You may be very sensitive about references to your loss. On the other hand, you might feel isolated if it seems that your friends are

When you are grieving, you may want to be alone. However, maintaining social ties can help you return to feeling normal.

excluding you. If that's the case, it may be that they are nervous about bringing up painful subjects. Try not to judge your friends during this time; they are probably grieving, too. Remember that anger is one of the stages of grief for many people, and try to avoid taking out your anger on them. If someone inadvertently says something insensitive, remind yourself that they're probably trying their best to help and did not mean to upset you.

Don't feel guilty about getting on with your life. You might feel bad about having fun at a party, since your friend can no longer share your happiness. You might feel disloyal when you spend time with friends and make new friends. This is not a betrayal. Your friend will always have a special place in your heart, even as you look toward the future.

Professional Help

Sometimes it's too difficult to work through grief on your own. Bereavement depression is a normal part of grieving, but grief can trigger clinical depression. Do you have frequent trouble sleeping? Have you gained or lost a significant amount of weight? Are you overwhelmed by simple or routine tasks? Have you cut yourself off from family and friends? Are you unable to feel happy about anything? Do you deaden your pain with drugs or alcohol? Have you thought about taking your own life? If any of these are true, you should consider contacting a psychotherapist to help you come to terms with your loss. You can also seek out grief support groups. Check with your school, church, or doctor for resources in your area, or look for groups online.

When a mutual friend is gone forever, getting together can be awkward. It's hard to know what to say and do.

Psychotherapy

Psychotherapy comes in many forms. In general, psychotherapy is a process in which a patient talks with a mental health professional about relationships, mental health conditions, or emotional issues, such as dealing with grief. The therapist, a person with specialized training in treating psychological conditions, uses various techniques. These might include reassurance, insight, persuasion, and information. It is hoped that the therapist can help you see yourself and your problem in a new and different way, so that you can deal with it more effectively.

Does talking about problems really help? The answer is yes—it does. No one knows exactly why this happens, but have you noticed that when you talk about something that's bothering you, you feel better afterwards? Most often you probably talk to a close friend or family member about problems or the things on your mind. But when a friend has died, that might not be enough. You may need more intense help or a more objective person to talk to. The decision to reach out to a professional for support and guidance can be one of the best and most important decisions of your life.

Support Groups

A support group is made up of people who share a common experience or concern and come together to give each other emotional or moral support. You could have a group with as few as two people, but most groups are larger. They may be local, national, or international. They can also be real or virtual (online).

As a teen, your grieving process is different from a child's or an adult's. A support group attended by other teens is often a good type of therapy.

Support groups usually have structure and often involve a mental health professional, a guest speaker, or planned events. Sometimes participants exchange only first names. Almost always, the group members promise that what they discuss in the meeting stays in the room; they do not share this information with others outside the group. Meetings are confidential.

In a grief support group, you will probably share thoughts and feelings about your friend's death and the way it is affecting you. It can be very comforting to hear from others who have gone through a similar experience. Being with others in support groups helps people feel less alone as they face their loss.

Post-Traumatic Stress Disorder

Some people suffer grief so intensely that they develop a condition called post-traumatic stress disorder (PTSD). If you were involved in a death-causing accident or witnessed it, you may be at risk for developing PTSD. People who lose someone suddenly may also develop PTSD because the death came as such a shock. Symptoms of PTSD can include severe anxiety, panic attacks, flashbacks that cause you to relive an event, terrible nightmares, general numbness, and fear. These symptoms may be so vivid and intense that you may not be able to do things you normally do. In addition to psychological stress, PTSD can cause headaches, stomachaches, dizziness, and other physical ailments.

Millions of people experience PTSD. If you are grieving and find yourself extremely stressed, anxious, or panicked, and if the symptoms interrupt your ability to live your life, you may have PTSD. It is very important for you to see a medical professional to help you manage your anxiety. In addition to therapy, some of the ways that people control PTSD and help themselves relax include meditating, stretching, deep breathing, exercising, or just talking to an understanding person. These techniques can help you calm yourself and help you cope with grief.

Grief is a process that takes time and requires effort. You will not wake up one morning and find that your grief has magically

Post-traumatic stress disorder results from feelings of anxiety and fear that may occur if you witnessed a friend's death.

Ten Great Questions to Ask a Counselor or Therapist About Dealing with the Death of a Friend

1 I've heard that it helps to keep a grief journal. What sort of things should I write about?

2 What can I do to sleep better at night?

3 I don't have an appetite. Is there any way to make it easier for me to eat?

4 I feel angry all the time, but I don't want to hurt my friends. How can I find an outlet for my anger?

5 How can I get over feelings of fear or panic?

6 I never had a chance to apologize to my friend for something I did. Is there some way I can make up for it?

7 My grades are going down because I can't concentrate. How can I get back on track with my schoolwork?

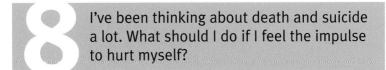

8 I've been thinking about death and suicide a lot. What should I do if I feel the impulse to hurt myself?

9 What can I do to show how special my friend was to me?

10 How can I help my family and friends with their grief?

disappeared. After your loss, you might find it excruciating to resume school, face your friends, and take up your daily routine once again. Gradually, however, you will discover that you're beginning to enjoy life again. There will be times when your grief returns. Day by day, though, you will work your way toward healing and acceptance of your loss.

four

WHAT CAN PEOPLE DO TO RECONNECT?

When teens experience loss, they often receive the most comfort from their friends. Your friends already play a vital role in your life. It's only natural that they will become an important source of support after your loss and that you offer comfort to your grieving friends. You could even sustain your connection to the friend you have lost by reaching out to his or her family.

Reaching Out to Mutual Friends

You might be unsure of how to act around a friend who is grieving. You do not want your friend to feel that you are uncomfortable around him or her, or that your friend cannot count on you in tough times. Should you try to resume your relationship as it was before the death of your mutual friend? What sort of things should you say?

What should you avoid saying? What should you do if your friend seems unable to cope with loss?

Sometimes it is too early in the grieving process to try to make your friend feel better. The best thing you can do is be supportive and understanding. Grief counselors suggest expressing honest and simple thoughts and emotions, such as:

- "I'm sorry."
- "I care."
- "I know you're hurting."
- "I wish I could share your pain."
- "I'm here for you."

Avoid using superficial or clichéd statements. You might be trying to help, but trite expressions may only frustrate your friend. Here are a few statements you should avoid:

- "I know how you feel." It's impossible to know exactly how someone else's grief feels.
- "He or she is in a better place now." That thought may not offer much comfort to a grieving friend, who might not subscribe to your religious beliefs.
- "Call me if you need anything." It's important to let your friend know that you're available if he or she needs support, but your friend might be too drained by grief to get in touch. Offer to stop by to help out with chores or errands.
- "You'll get over it." That's no comfort to someone who is grieving.

When there are no words to say to a mourning friend, a hug is a good way to show you care. Just being there is important.

➡ "It was God's will." People have different religious beliefs that should be honored.

Let your friend mourn in his or her own way. The most crucial thing you can do is to simply be there when he or she needs you. Help with the simple tasks. People in the first stages of grief tend to have trouble focusing on day-to-day concerns. They have more important things on their minds than laundry and dirty dishes. Offer to do these tasks for them, or simply do them without being asked. Bring home your friend's assignments and books if he or she is absent from school.

If your friend would like you to, serve an important role by letting others know that someone close to your friend has died. This will help them to prepare themselves for your friend's grief. Carrying this news also means carrying a serious responsibility. Dramatic events, such as when someone is killed, are commonly a source of rumors and exaggerations. People add more drama to the story as they pass it from one to another. Tell only the facts that you know are true, and make them as simple and plain as possible to help squelch rumors. Also, be sensitive. Your friend may not want some details revealed. Respect his or her privacy.

Your friend might want to talk about loss and grief. On the other hand, he or she might find it too painful to put into words right away. Give your friend a break. If he or she is angry or overwrought, understand that this is an expression of grief and it is not directed at you. Let your friend cry, express anger, or share thoughts and feelings. Offer memories and stories about your mutual friend who died. Don't try to give advice on how to cope unless your friend asks.

Try sharing some of the things that help you manage your grief, but remember that the path to healing is different for everyone. Are there any books, poems, or songs that helped you to cope with your grief? Did you find that writing or art projects helped you to express your feelings? Put together a photo collage and share it with your friends. Once you return to school, you can help friends with schoolwork and participate in extracurricular activities together.

Everybody has his or her own response to loss. Some of your friends may seem to bounce back immediately. Some may draw closer to you, while others may need space to grieve. Don't take it personally if someone distances himself or herself from you after the death of a mutual friend. A traumatic loss sometimes changes us or changes our relationships with other people. Your friend may renew your friendship after working through the process of grieving.

You may realize that a friend is having trouble coping with his or her grief. Make sure your friend knows that you are there to help in whatever way you can. If you get worried about your friend's well-being after a loss, suggest that he or she consider seeing a counselor or therapist. If you notice risky or self-destructive behavior in a friend, tell one of your friend's parents, a school counselor, a teacher, or other trusted adult about your concern. Don't feel guilty about "betraying" your friend. You're showing true friendship by getting help for someone who cannot help himself or herself.

No two people will grieve the same way. Give your friend the freedom to express her or his feelings, and try to be accepting.

Reaching Out to Your Friend's Family

It's a good idea to pay a visit to your friend's family. They will be glad to see you. You might represent a connection to their child who has died. It is incredibly difficult for a parent to lose a child. In the usual order of things, children are supposed to live longer than their parents, so it is a particular shock to experience the death of a child. Also, parents feel a natural responsibility for their child's well-being. They often feel guilt for not doing anything to prevent the death, even though there is usually no rational reason for this guilt. Your friend's siblings will also be feeling shock and grief at losing a brother or sister. All of a sudden, their role within the family is drastically changed.

Let your friend's parents know how special their son or daughter was to you. Write a letter of condolence expressing how much the friendship meant to you. Take along copies of photographs of your friend. Offer to spend time with your friend's siblings. Ask if there's any way you can help with the funeral or memorial planning, or if you can pitch in around the house. Maybe you can help out by babysitting your friend's younger siblings.

Invite your friend's parents to attend events that your friend would have participated in, such as a band concert, school play, or graduation. They might be glad to have this opportunity for continuity in their lives. On the other hand, don't be hurt if they feel unable to handle such painful reminders of their loss.

Over time, grief will become easier to bear. Your friends, and the family of your friend who has died, will go through the process of healing and acceptance. Throughout the process, let them know that you're there for them. You may even find that your own grief eases as you help others come to terms with their loss.

WHEN WILL I RECOVER?

There is no clear-cut path to recovery from grief. Little by little, you will begin to realize that you are able to resume and enjoy the everyday activities and notable events of your life. You can dwell on memories of your friend without feeling sad. You're able to concentrate on studying for tests, and you can become absorbed in interesting projects for class. You find yourself laughing and making jokes. You no longer have trouble sleeping, and you're maintaining a healthy diet. You're able to enjoy your social life again. You make plans for the weekend—and for your long-term future. Still, there are days when grief and the accompanying feelings of anger and sadness return. Sometimes these feelings will pass quickly; other times, they may really take hold of you. Remember that healing from grief does not mean you will never again feel sad about losing your friend. It just means you have come to terms with your loss.

As you recover from losing a friend, loneliness and frustration will become less intense and will occur less frequently.

Emotional Reminders and Special Occasions

Specific reminders of your friend will open floodgates of memories and emotions. Your friend's favorite songs, certain places where you and your friend spent time, even particular pieces of clothing—these types of triggers may bring back intense feelings of grief and loss. In time, however, reminders of your friend will no longer bring so much pain.

Special occasions and important milestones in your life may also serve as reminders of your loss. When Christmas comes around, for example, you might feel pain at the thought that this is the first Christmas without your friend. You might see something that would have been a great Christmas present for your friend. You may still be too drained by grief to enjoy the holiday season. New Year's could be difficult for you because it decisively puts last year's events—including the death of your friend—in the past, and you might still have trouble distancing yourself from your loss. If you lost a boyfriend or girlfriend, Valentine's Day might seem agonizingly lonely. Your friend's birthday and the anniversary of his or her death will call attention to your loss once again.

Make a mental note in advance that these might be difficult days for you. For each occasion, find a special way to remember your friend. On his or her birthday, for example, you could mark the day with your friend's favorite cake, complete with candles. Or, if your friend was buried in a cemetery, you could visit the grave each year to refresh your memories of the good times you had together.

Strong emotions can be unleashed upon hearing a friend's recorded voice or when listening to music that held special significance for you.

Ways to Honor Your Friend

Sometime after the death of your friend, you may suddenly realize that a couple days have gone by that you haven't had a single thought about your friend. Don't feel guilty or worry that this is a betrayal of his or her memory. It is a natural part of the process of moving forward with your own life and letting go.

Letting go doesn't mean that you must put the memory of your friend out of your mind. After you're past the initial shock of his or her death, you may find an outlet for your grief in planning ways to pay tribute to your friend.

Take part in organizing a memorial service for your friend. A memorial service is often less formal than a funeral. It can take place anytime after the funeral, from a few days to months later. Sometimes families choose to hold annual memorial services for a loved one. Choose a passage from a book, a poem, or a piece of your own writing that you can read aloud at the service.

Maybe you want to get involved in an organization that works to prevent tragedy from befalling other teenagers. Students Against Destructive Decisions (SADD), for example, has this mission statement: "To provide students with the best prevention and intervention tools possible to deal with the issues of underage drinking, other drug use, impaired driving, and other destructive decisions."

You might want to participate in an organization that works toward suicide awareness and prevention. Perhaps you'd be interested in supporting education and fund-raising for a particular medical condition, such as cancer or AIDS.

To honor a friend who has died, make regular visits to the cemetery to beautify the gravesite and dwell on his or her memory.

10 FACTS ABOUT WHEN A FRIEND DIES

1 There is no single "right" reaction to the loss of a friend.

2 Funerals and other rituals give teens a chance to share their grief with others.

3 Grief is not a choice. It is the emotional response to a loss.

4 There is no fixed timetable for grieving.

5 Denial, anger, guilt, and depression are all normal parts of the grieving process.

6 When teens experience loss, they often receive the most comfort from their friends.

7 A grieving teen might have trouble concentrating and juggling school, family life, and extracurricular activities.

8 A counselor or therapist can help teens come to terms with loss.

9 A grief support group gives teens a chance to talk about their thoughts, feelings, and memories with others who understand the pain of loss.

10 Specific reminders of a deceased friend will open floodgates of memories and emotions.

Paying tribute to your friend does not have to be a public matter. You can also remember your friend with small, personal gestures. If your friend played soccer, for example, attend a soccer game. When you go to one of your friend's favorite restaurants, order a dish that your friend particularly liked. Spend time by your friend's grave, and find a way to make it meaningful. Maybe you could tell your friend about the latest news in your life. Take along flowers that you think your friend would appreciate.

Now that you've personally endured the process of grief, you might consider joining or starting a grief support group at your school. A grief support group is made up of your peers who have also experienced loss in their lives. It gives teens a chance to talk about their thoughts, feelings, and memories with others who understand the pain of loss.

You also may want to organize an informal support group among your friends who all knew the friend you lost. Perhaps

When you recover from your grief, the flavor returns to life. Once again, you'll be able to smile and laugh easily with your friends.

you could plan a memorial activity on the anniversary of his or her death. You might plant a tree or flower bed in your friend's memory, or paint a mural of a scene that would have been special to your friend. If your friend was passionate about a particular cause, you could dedicate the day to volunteer work for that cause.

As you let go and move on, reminders of your friend will begin to evoke memories of the good times you had together. You realize that you will be able to feel happiness again. Reminiscences may be bittersweet, but they will no longer bring pain. Perhaps in working through your grief, you found an inner strength you didn't know you had. Maybe you learned something new about friendship, compassion, and living life to the fullest.

agonizing Very painful.

anguish Extreme pain or distress.

bereavement State of sorrow and loneliness over the death or departure of a friend or loved one.

condolences Expressions of sympathy.

deceased Dead; one who has died.

denial Refusal to accept or admit the reality of a situation or experience.

depressant Drug that reduces excitability.

depression Mental state often marked by sadness, inactivity, an inability to concentrate, and thoughts of suicide.

grief Suffering arising from bereavement.

hospice Facility designed to take care of the terminally ill.

internalize To make internal or personal.

lethargy State of inactivity or lack of energy.

mortality State or quality of being mortal, or human and subject to death.

mourning Outward expression of grief.

ordeal Severe trial or experience.

overwrought Extremely excited or agitated.

phenomenon Significant fact or event.

psychotherapist One who treats mental or emotional disorders.

ritual Series of actions or words performed in a prescribed
manner, especially as part of a formal ceremony.

shiva In Judaism, the weeklong period of formal mourning
following the death of a close relative.

stimulant Drug that temporarily increases physiological and
metabolic activity of the body.

terminal illness Disease or disorder that cannot be cured; illness
that ends only in death.

therapy Treatment of a physical or mental disorder.

traumatic Emotionally stressful.

wake Ceremony during which a vigil is held over the body of
a dead person, prior to burial.

Comfort Zone Camp
2101-A Westmoreland Street
Richmond, VA 23230
(866) 488-5679
Web site: http://www.comfortzonecamp.org
Holds camps for children ages seven to seventeen from across the country who have experienced the death of a loved one.

Dougy Center for Grieving Children & Families
P.O. Box 86852
Portland, OR 97286
(503) 775-5683 (Toll free: (866) 775-5683)
Web site: http://www.dougy.org
The first center in the United States to provide peer support groups for grieving children. Its mission is to provide support in a safe place where children, teens, and their families grieving a death can share their experiences as they move forward.

Fernside: A Center for Grieving Children
4380 Malsbary Road, Suite 300
Cincinnati, OH 45242
(513) 745-0111
Web site: http://www.fernside.org

A not-for-profit, non-denominational organization serving grieving children and their families.

GriefNet.org—Where Grace Happens
P.O. Box 3272
Ann Arbor, MI 48106-3272
Web sites: http://www.griefnet.org; http://www.kidsaid.com
   Online resources that provide support for people working through loss and grief issues of all kinds.

Rainbows—Restoring Hope to Grieving Youth
2100 Golf Road #370
Rolling Meadows, IL 60008
(800) 266-3206
Web site: http://www.rainbows.org
   An international, not-for-profit organization that fosters emotional healing among children grieving a loss from a life-altering crisis.

Web Sites

Due to the changing nature of Internet links, Rosen Publishing has developed an online list of Web sites related to the subject of this book. This site is updated regularly. Please use this link to access the list:

http://www.rosenlinks.com/faq/whfd

Bowen, Deborah E., and Susan L. Strickler. *A Good Friend for Bad Times: Helping Others Through Grief.* Minneapolis, MN: Augsburg Books, 2004.

Deits, Bob. *Life After Loss: A Practical Guide to Renewing Your Life After Experiencing Major Loss*, Fourth ed. Cambridge, MA: Lifelong Books, 2004.

Dower, Laura. *I Will Remember You: What to Do When Someone You Love Dies—A Guidebook Through Grief for Teens.* New York, NY: Scholastic, Inc., 2001.

Fitzgerald, Helen. *The Grieving Teen: A Guide for Teenagers and Their Friends.* New York, NY: Fireside Books, 2000.

Gravelle, Karen. *Teenagers Face to Face with Bereavement.* New York, NY: iUniverse, 2000.

Grollman, Earl A. *Straight Talk About Death for Teenagers: How to Cope with Losing Someone You Love.* Boston, MA: Beacon Press, 1993.

Kübler-Ross, Elisabeth, and David Kessler. *On Grief and Grieving: Finding the Meaning of Grief Through the Five Stages of Loss.* New York, NY: Scribner, 2005.

Yoshimoto, Banana. *Kitchen.* New York, NY: Washington Square Press, 1993.

Bibliography

Bowen, Deborah E., and Susan L. Strickler. *A Good Friend for Bad Times: Helping Others Through Grief.* Minneapolis, MN: Augsburg Books, 2004.

Deits, Bob. *Life After Loss: A Practical Guide to Renewing Your Life After Experiencing Major Loss,* Fourth ed. Cambridge, MA: Lifelong Books, 2004.

Fitzgerald, Helan. *The Mourning Handbook: A Complete Guide for the Bereaved.* New York, NY: Simon and Schuster, 1994.

Kübler-Ross, Elisabeth, and David Kessler. *On Grief and Grieving: Finding the Meaning of Grief Through the Five Stages of Loss.* New York, NY: Scribner, 2005.

Shaw, Eva. *What to Do When a Loved One Dies: A Practical and Compassionate Guide to Dealing with Death on Life's Terms.* Irvine, CA: Dickens Press, 1994.

Index

A

acceptance, as a grief stage, 6, 14, 17, 19, 21, 37, 45, 46
ailments, 9, 34
anger, as a grief stage, 17, 18, 30, 36, 41, 46, 52

B

bargaining, as a grief stage, 17, 18
bereavement depression, 30
burial services, 12

C

cancer, 9
cemeteries, 5, 12, 48
clinical depression, 30
condolences, 12, 44
confidential, 33
confusion, as a response to death, 9, 24
counselors, 10, 27, 39, 42, 52

D

denial, as a grief stage, 7, 17–18, 52
depression/despair, as a grief stage, 17, 18–19, 52
drug/alcohol use, as a way to cope with a friend's death, 27–28, 30

E

emotional triggers, 48, 53, 55
explaining death to teenagers, 4–6

F

funerals/death rituals, 5–6, 12, 14, 50, 52

G

grief
   affecting friendships, 25, 28, 30, 38–39, 41–42, 52
   coping with, 6, 25, 27–28, 30, 32, 34
   counseling for, 12, 27, 39
   effects on health, 16, 25, 27, 34, 36, 46
   five stages of, 16–19, 21, 30, 41
   isolation, as a reaction to, 5, 15, 28, 30
   and loss of appetite, 27, 36, 46
   myths and facts about, 22, 24
   as a natural process, 6, 7, 16, 22, 34, 52
   "right" forms of, 7, 21, 24, 52
   and self-destructive behavior, 27–28, 42
   support groups for, 30, 32–34, 53
guilt, as a response to death, 11, 21, 24, 50, 52

H

healing process, 12, 14, 37, 45
honoring a deceased friend, 50, 53, 55
hospices, 9, 10
humanistic services, 12

I

internalize, 27
invincibility, teens' sense of, 4

K

Kübler-Ross, Elisabeth, 17, 18

L

lethargy, 18

M

memorial services, 44, 50
mortality, 11

N

numbness, as a response to death, 7, 18, 34

O

On Grief and Grieving, 16–17

P

post-traumatic stress disorder (PTSD), 34
psychiatrists, 17
psychologists, 12
psychotherapists, 12, 30, 32

Q

questions to ask a counselor/ therapist about dealing with the death of a friend, 36–37

R

reaching out to deceased friend's family, 44–45
remembrance, 12

S

self-critical, 18
sex, as a way to cope with a friend's death, 28
shock, as a response to death, 4, 7, 9, 44, 50
sitting shiva, 12
Students Against Destructive Decisions (SADD), 50

T

terminal illness, 9, 10
therapists, 42, 52
tragedy, 4

U

"uppers," 28

W

wake, 12
what not to say to a grieving friend, 21, 22, 39, 41, 42
when a friend dies
  from a gradual illness, 4, 9–10
  from a sudden illness, 4, 9
  from suicide, 4, 11
  ten facts about, 52–53
  from violence, 4, 10–11

Photo Credits

Designer: Evelyn Horovicz; **Editor:** Christopher Roberts
Photo Researcher: Marty Levick